A Witch Among The Herbs

Materia Magicka
of Herbs, Flowers, and Trees

❧

Spells

❧

Craftings and More

Ilana Sturm

PENDRAIG

Pendraig Publishing, Inc
Green Valley Lake, CA 92341

©Ilana Sturm 2016.
All rights reserved.

Layout and Design:
Miss D's Designs, LLC

Cover Design:
Miss D's Designs, LLC

Published 2016

Printed in the United States of America

ISBN: 978-1-936922-85-7

In Grateful Appreciation to

Peter Paddon in the Summerlands

Linda Paddon

and

Raven Womack

with

Thanks and Blessings

Introduction

As you open this Herbal Materia Magicka you will
find that a world of possibilities awaits you. Within
its pages you will find many secrets, some that
are not usually shared until a person has attained
a certain level of magickal ability. As with all
magicks – it is upon the user to make proper use of
the knowledge given. Use it well and with wisdom
and discernment.

Part One of this book contains the Materia
Magicka. We all know that herbs can be both
medicinal and curative, however for the purposes
of this book I have listed only their magickal
properties and how best to use them in an easy and
straightforward manner.

They should, therefore, not be consumed but rather
carried, sprinkled, used in spell crafting and mojo
bags. Made into washes and baths, used as inks,
hung from windows, doors and hearths or burned
on a charcoal block as an incense along with a
myriad of other ways that can be found to use them.

You may note as you read through that many of the herbs have multiple uses and some even share the same attributes. Herbal magick, like crystals, works on a subtle, vibratory level. Magick itself being all about intent, focus and the ability of the student, adept or witch to channel the magickal energies.

No two Materia Magickas will be exactly the same because no two witches are exactly the same. Most experienced witches prefer to 'tweak' a magickal recipe to their own personal taste, but will use the basics as a starting point.

Therefore, find the herb, flower or tree that works best for you; it may be the one that is the least expensive, easiest to grow or the one that can be found at the local herb market.

If you can't get a particular herb, scroll through this book, you are sure to find another that can do the job just as well.

For the experienced practitioner I wish you joy and success in using this book and hope that you can add to your own herbal repertoire from mine.

After 40 years on the crooked path, through traditional witchcraft and then many years as a solitary, studying eastern and western mystery traditions, herbal and crystal magicks and from a family tradition of three generations who practiced Celtic folk magick, I like to think that I picked up a thing or two along the way.

For those who are more recent additions to magick or the craft of the wise, I will give you some words of wisdom, learned after trial and error and many years of practice – "keep it simple!"

Magick is everywhere, it lurks in the shadows and the 'tween places, you can't do anything more with 50 herbs than you can with 3 or 4. Remember intent, focus and channel are the keys. Herbs, crystals, wands and potions etcetera, are just the tools we use to harness, expand and project our powers. So if your intent is clear and your mind is focussed on the task at hand, you will easily channel the mystical energies and be successful in all that you do.

The crafting section of this book is close to my heart. As an esoteric artist, scribe for a magickal coven and craft teacher, I can tell you that there is nothing more powerful than a charm, book, tool or implement made by hand, with all the love and magick that you alone can imprint and imbue within it, not to mention the fact that it brings with it a great deal of joy and satisfaction.

Contents

Materia Magicka

of Herbs, Flowers, and Trees

By the sun and moon at night

by the flickering candle's light

cast a circle thrice around

may light and love and joy be found

At this time and in this place

in this very special space

Magicks fly and come to me

as I will, so mote it be

Ilana

A̶grimony

Agrimonia Eupatoria
(Cockleburr, Sticklewort)

DISPEL NEGATIVITY, WARD OFF A HEX

RETURN TO SENDER

A very powerful herb

Use to dissipate negative energies

by carrying in a black mojo bag

To ward off a hex or curse

and return to sender

burn the herb with white sage incense

and cast the powdered remains

to the wind

$\mathcal{A}$lum
Aluminum Sulfate

POWER AND POSITIVITY

Use Alum in your magickal inks
for an added boost of power
and to remove any negative
thoughts as you scribe

Alum is a great absorber of
negative energy and will work
wonders when placed in a bowl
in a room where there is
depression, anger or negativity

*A*lum Root

Geranium Maculatum
(Cranesbill, Herb Robert)

PROTECTION FOR HOME AND SELF

Infuse the herb in hot water
and let stand for three hours then
sprinkle the infusion around the home

For personal protection
add the infusion to a bath

Place parts of the herb beneath
the bed to protect during sleep

*A*ngelica

Angelica Archangelica
(Archangel, Masterwort)

CALL AN ANGEL

PURIFY AND PROTECT

Drives away negative energies

A very potent purification herb

Defeats malicious entities

Protects against psychic attack

Use when calling an Angel,

Guardian Angel or Archangel

Place the herb in a mojo bag

White to call an Angel

Purple to protect

Place under your pillow at night

Carry during the day

or sprinkle directly into the cauldron

for a 'working' spell

*A*nise Seed

Pimpinella Anisum
(Aniseed)

ROMANCE, JOY AND UNITY

Use at a Handfasting instead of rice
Anise Seed will promote romance
and joy in each others company

Shamans should burn with incense
before astral journeys to protect
both the physical and astral bodies
and to ensure a safe return
as Anise Seed is a great spiritual uniter

Asafoetida

Ferula Foetida
(Devil's Dung)

REMOVE A HEX

STOP PSYCHIC ATTACK

This age old magickal herb will

do more than ward off a curse or hex

it will demolish it!

Along with evil spirits and psychic attacks

Place in a small red mojo bag

and hang from your main entry door

or sprinkle directly onto a written spell

to do the trick

*A*sh Tree and Leaves
Fraxinus Excelsior

LOVE AND LUCK

PART OF THE FAERY TRIAD

Dry and grind into a powder
Then carry in a pink velvet bag
to attract love and luck your way

Along with Oak and Hawthorn
this tree is sacred to the Fey (Faery Folk)
Scatter the leaves within the circle
to attract Faeries and Elementals
or use for Faery gifts and blessings

$\mathcal{B}$alm of Gilead

Populus -.
(Poplar Buds)

CAN BE USED TO MANIFEST
AND TO HEAL

Carry on your person to exude and attract love

or to manifest your wants and needs

Helps to heal a broken heart

and lead you to a new love

*B*ats *Wing Herb*

Ilex spp.
(Holly, Yerba Mate, Winterberry)

TO BIND ANOTHER'S POWER

Place the herb in a bowl

with their picture

Then cover with earth

Recite a binding spell that includes

the specific behaviour you want to stop

then bury in the garden

Bay Leaf
Laurus Nobilis

TO CREATE AND INSPIRE

For artists, musicians and writers
Keep a Bay Leaf next to your writing inks
or painting materials

For musicians use the Bay Leaves like an
incense smudge around your instruments
to keep your creativity flowing
and a Muse close by for inspiration

*B*ayberry

Myrica Cerifera
(Wax Myrtle)

**AN ALL ROUND EXCELLENT HERB
FOR PROMOTING
GOOD VIBES, LUCK, PROSPERITY
AND A HAPPY HOME**

Place in the home, near the hearth

to create calm and harmony

Carry in a green mojo bag to promote wealth

Use in all spells that require a peaceful

solution and an end to arguments

*B*earberry

Arctostaphylos Uva-ursi
(Uva-Ursi)

Use when scrying

or when attempting any psychic work

Will sharpen your intuitive abilities

Often used by Shamans

as an aid in clear seeing

Burn as an incense

$\mathcal{B}$elladonna

Atropa Belladonna
(Deadly Nightshade, Banewort,
Witch's Berry and Sorcerer's Berry)

HIGHLY TOXIC POISON

NEVER INGEST

Use as an ink in Love spells

Ruled by the moon

Belladonna was used to induce trance
states and was the chief ingredient
in medieval flying ointments

Use Mugwort instead

Benzoin Gum

Styrax Benzoin
(Friar's Balsam)

OFTEN USED IN INCENSE
AS A BINDING AGENT

Benzoin will increase memory

and promote wisdom

helping to open the mind to new

thoughts and ideas

$\mathcal{B}$ergamot

Mentha Citrata
(Horsemint, Lemon Mint)

MONEY AND SUCCESS

To ensure your purse or wallet is never empty

carry some inside and rub some on the outside

Add to your cauldron when spell casting

for all matters of success or gain

Betony

*Betonica officinalis; Stachys Betonica,
Syn, Stachys officinalis
(Wood Betony, Bishopswort)*

USE FOR PROTECTION AND PURIFICATION

Particularly good for problems in sleeping

Make a small herb pillow to place

underneath your pillow at night

to help drive away nightmares

Use when circle casting outside

to protect and purify the area

$\mathcal{B}$irch

Betula spp.

PROTECTION

Use the bark from the tree
which has highly protective energies

Break into small pieces and
add to a pouch before hanging
from the front and rear doors
of your home

Remember to thank the tree
and give it a moment to
remove its energy
before you take the bark

Black Cohosh

Actaea Racemose
(Black Snakeroot)

POWER BOOST

FERTILITY

A highly potent and magickal herb

Use to boost the power of spells

by adding to oils and potions

when mixing

Soak in a bath for fertility

Bladderwrack

Fucus Vesiculosis
(Herb of the Sea, Sea Spirit, Sea Oak)

Spirits that abound in the Sea

are attracted to this herb

For Business Owners

bring in more sales and attract clientele

by infusing the herb in hot water

when cool, sprinkle around the shop

or workplace and wipe your front door

with the infusion

$\mathcal{B}$lessed Thistle

Cnicus Benedictus
(Holy Thistle)

ENERGIZING

Place near the bedside of one who
has been ill to help regain strength

PROTECTIVE

Keep some in the home as it is
detrimental to thieves

Sacred to Pan who protects the woodlands

$\mathcal{B}$oneset

Eupatorium Perfoliatum
(Indian Sage)

REMOVES NEGATIVITY

Great for dispelling built up negative

energies, particularly in the home

or when moving to a new home

Burn as an incense

or make a herbal tea infusion

to sprinkle in each room

$\mathcal{B}$orage

Borago Officinalis
(Peace Herb, Starflower)

COURAGE APLENTY,
PEACE AND GOOD JUDGEMENT

When courage is needed

carry the herb with you in a

red binding or mojo bag

When you need good judgement

make a herbal amulet or burn as incense

$\mathcal{B}$uckeyes

Aesculus Hippocastanum
(Horse Chestnut)

ATTRACTS MONEY

Carry the Chestnut in a
green pouch to which you have added
a gold or silver coin

Write out a money gathering spell
and wrap it around the Buckeye
to place in your purse or pocket

$\mathcal{B}$ugle

Ajuga spp.
(Bugleweed)

DREAMS OF THE FUTURE, VISION QUESTS AND SÉANCES

Make a herbal tea infusion

When cool, place a dot upon your 3rd eye

and across your temples

or burn with Amber incense during rituals

$\mathcal{B}$urdock Root

Arctium Lappa
(Bat Weed)

PROTECTS AND PURIFIES

Add directly to the mix
when creating herbal spell pouches
or for any spellcrafting that requires a
protective element

Will clear the mind and ready for vision quests

Calamus Root
Acorus Calamus
(Sweet Flag)

ATTRACTS LOVE

STRENGTHENS SPELLS

DISSIPATES BAD ENERGIES

Chop and sprinkle into potions

Or add to written spells

Brings a positive resolution if

added to incense and burned

Calendula
Calendula Officinalis
(Marigold)

AIDS IN CLAIRVOYANCE

Dry the flowers

then add to a herb pillow

or place directly beneath your pillow

at night for clairvoyant dreams

and for vitality the next morning

Cardamom

Elletaria Cardamomum

LOVE AND PASSION

Grind the seeds and add to a love potion
or make a herbal love pouch by adding the seeds
and rose petals to a pink mojo bag for love
and red for passion

Add to formulas for inspiration

Cascara Sagrada

Rhamnus Purshiana
(Sacred Bark)

USE TO CONSECRATE MAGICKAL TOOLS

BRING GOOD FORTUNE

WIN A COURT CASE OR PROVE A POINT

Soak and add to a small potion bottle

Use to wipe over magickal tools

Or carry the potion with you

and sprinkle contents where required

Cassia Bark

Cinnamomum Cassia

ATTRACTS PROSPERITY AND LOVE

Add to spells and potions

or mojo bags:

pink for love and green for prosperity

*C*atnip
Nepeta Cataria
(Catwort)

CALL A CAT FAMILIAR
AND CREATE A BOND

Plant the herb near your door

In olden days a sprig of catnip would be
hung above the door to usher in good luck!

A mild hallucinatory if inhaled as an incense
it is sometimes used for psychic endeavours
like vision quests

Cayenne Pepper

Capsicum Annum
(Guinea Pepper, Red Pepper)

PROSPERITY AND SPEED

Add a pinch to all magickal workings
that require a speedy result

This herb is often used in Voodoo
and Santeria

Great when added to a spell
pouch or mojo bag
to attract prosperity

Cedarwood

Calocedrus spp., Cedrus spp.,
Juniperus Virginiana, Thuja spp.,
Toona Ciliata
(Summer Solstice Herb)

BLESS AND ATTRACT

Burn as an incense at Naming

Ceremonies or Wiccanings

Cedarwood will bless and attract good fortune

Also use to cleanse and consecrate

the Witch's Wand

just pass the Wand through the smoke

while you chant

Chamomile
Roman-Anthemis Nobilis
German-Matricaria Recutita

TO PROMOTE A RESTFUL NIGHTS SLEEP

Dry the flowers and place in a sleep pillow

For headaches
Mix with lavender flowers and place the
sleep pillow over the eyes as you rest

Chaparral
Larrea Tridentada
(Creosote Bush)

PROTECTION

When casting circle sprinkle the herb
around the outer edge for extra protection

Burn as an incense to alter
a run of bad luck

Excellent for use with potions and spells
that require an extra boost of protection

*C*hickory Root
Cichorium Intybus
(Coffee Weed, Chicory Root)

Soak and make a tea

This can then be used to cleanse

and consecrate your Magickal Tools

Cards, Crystals, Athames, Wands, Tarot Decks, etc

*C*innamon
Cinnamomum Zeylanicum
(Sweetwood)

CLAIRVOYANCE AND ATUNEMENT

WELCOMING

Use the powder, bark or sticks

Add powder to a charcoal block and burn as
incense to enhance clairvoyance

Chop the bark and carry in a mojo bag

Bind the sticks with a lavender ribbon
and place in the home to welcome

Cinquefoil
Potentilla spp.
(Five Finger Grass)

LOVE, MONEY, PROTECTION,
SUCCESS, SPIRITUALITY

THE FIVE GOALS OF MOST PEOPLE

This herb is powered by the full moon

To bless and protect

Carry in a purple velvet or satin bag

and tie with a green string or ribbon

on the first Monday of a full moon

Clover

Trifolium Pratense
(Red Clover)

USE IN A WORKING SPELL TO STRENGTHEN

AND TO OVERCOME OPPOSITION

MULTIPLY

Clover will offer you psychic protection

Sprinkle around the magickal area

you intend to read tarot cards or scry in

Clover will multiply any spell crafting

Clove

Syzygium Aromaticum

PROTECTION, REMOVES NEGATIVE VIBES

Great herb to stop gossip in its tracks

Anoint a candle with Clove oil

and burn with the gossip in mind

Keeps negative vibrations at bay

Use as an incense

Or carry on your person

Coltsfoot

Tussilago Farfara
(Coughwort)

PEACE AND LOVE

Add Coltsfoot to your love spells

Will bring harmony, tranquility and
peace to your meditation area

Make a herbal amulet or burn as an incense

Comfrey
Symphytum Uplandicum, Symphytum Officinale
(Bruisewort)

HEALING

SAFE TRAVEL

Place a little Comfrey in your travel bag
with a pinch of Mugwort to ensure a safe trip

Make a herbal amulet to hang in the car
when taking road trips

Add when crafting any sort of
healing spell or potion

Coriander

Coriandrum Sativum
(Chinese Parsley, Cilantro)

LOVE AND PASSION

Crush the seeds and carry in a

mojo bag

pink for love, red for passion

At night, place the bag

under your pillow

Cubeb Berries

Piper Cubeba
(Loveberry)

SPICE UP YOUR SEX LIFE

Add to incense and burn to attract
and arouse a lover

Add to love spells, pouches and sachets
to give them an extra kick

Damiana

Turnera Diffusa
Aphrodesiac

ADD TO A HERBAL BATH

Or burn on a charcoal block with your

favourite incense when you want

to turn up the heat

Dandelion Root

Taraxacum spp.
(Lion's Tooth)

THE WISHING HERB

Write your wish

then place into an envelope

Sprinkle in some of the herb

Seal and draw a pentacle on the front

Then burn and send the ashes to the

four winds

Devil's Bit

Scabiosa Succisa
(Scabious)

HIGHLY PROTECTIVE

For your home or person
Place in a black cloth
and tie with a black cord
to either carry or leave in the home

Light a black candle with a pentacle
scribed into it and sprinkle the herb
as you go through each room
to protect from a curse or hex

Devil's Claw

Harpagophytum

TO STOP EVIL IN ITS TRACKS

AND REMOVE NEGATIVE VIBES

Infuse the herb in hot water

Then top up with cold before washing

counters, shelves and doors in the home

Use a charcoal block and burn as incense

before get-togethers

Particularly good for gatherings

where larger groups may convene

Devil's Shoestring

Viburnum spp.
(Indian Currant)

PROBLEM SOLVER

Write your problem on a piece of parchment

Neatly fold and place in a glass

add a little of the chopped root

and half fill the glass with alcohol

Place out under the moon

As the alcohol evaporates, so does your problem

Next morning take a deep breath

and pour the potion into

the garden as you breathe out

Let it take your problems with it

$\mathcal{D}ill$

Anethum Graveolens

Add some Dill to your bath water and soak

Or add some to a salad and eat

to make someone find you irresistible

A very popular uncrossing herb

Dittany of Crete

Dictamus Origanoides

MANIFESTATION AND FOCUS

SPIRIT AND SÉANCE WORK

Need to manifest a job?

Money, love, friendship?

Carry in a mojo bag to help you

manifest your desire

Burn Dittany of Crete as an incense

during séances to help bring through 'spirit'

Dragon's Blood
Sanguis Draconis

POWER

Add to a working spell to give
extra power

Dragon's Blood when burned as an
incense is one of the most potent
uncrossing herbs

Used in magickal inks to create a truly
Red Dragon's Blood

Dragon's Tears

Scutellaria Costaricana
(Scarlet Scullcap)

DISPEL NEGATIVITY

WARD OFF HEXES AND CROSSINGS

Soak the herb and sprinkle

around the home or workplace

Or carry in a yellow mojo bag

*E*lder Tree and Berries
Sambucus spp.

PROTECTION, POWER, RELEASE

CONTACT ELEMENTALS

WANDS

Carry in a mojo bag on your person
This is a powerful protector for warding
off all forms of attack

Will release all spells made against you

Sit beneath an Elder Tree
and meditate on the Elementals
they will soon come to you!

Elecampane Root
Inula Helenium
(Elfwort)

TRUE LOVE, DIVINATION

Add to a charcoal block
some of the powdered root and burn
to enhance your psychic power

Carry in a pink mojo bag
with Rose petals and Vervain to
attract your true love

*E*yebright
Euphrasia Officinalis

CLAIRVOYANCE

Make a tea from the herb

When cool soak an eye pad with the mix

and place on the eyes for five minutes

to promote and enhance your astral vision

*F*ennel

Foeniculum Vulgare

PURIFY AND HEAL

WARD OFF NEGATIVE ENERGY

Add to working spells

where healing is required

Or to keep negative spirits at bay

place in a blue pouch and

hang from windows

Fenugreek

Trigonella Foenum-graecum

HERB FOR THE SUMMER SOLSTICE

HERB OF THE SUN

PROSPERITY

Add to incense and burn during
Solstice rituals

Place some seeds in with your
prosperity spells and potions

*F*everfew

Chrysanthemum Parthenium

MIDSUMMER DREAMS

COLDS, FLU

CREATES A RESTFUL SPACE

Carry in a yellow mojo bag

to keep bugs at bay

Burn to create peace and healing

Particularly good for meditation areas

$\mathcal{F}$rankincense

Olibanum spp.

DIVINATION, CONSECRATION, WISDOM,
STRENGTH, PROTECTION

Can be added to all spell crafting

potions or mojo bags for an extra boost

Great to burn as this is where we

get the name 'incense' from

Use to consecrate magickal tools and

to gain insight and wisdom on magickal journeys

Galangal Root

Alpinia spp.
(Lo John the Conqueror)

PROTECTION, HEALTH, LUCK

MAGICKAL LEARNING

Carry to protect the wearer

Soak and Sprinkle around the home
for all matters of magickal development

Burn on a charcoal block
to promote luck and good health

Gentian Root

Gentiana Lutea

POWER TO ALL SPELLS

LOVE, DESIRE, SENSUALITY

Add to cauldrons, mojo bags
and spells to bring an extra boost
of power

Particularly good for spreading love

Make a herbal amulet

$\mathcal{G}$inger

Zingiber Officinale

SUCCESS AND MONEY

Grind to a powder and add a pinch
or two to spells and potions
to increase the chance of success

During the full moon
add a pinch of Ginger to a written spell
or potion to attract money
Then carry with you

Ginseng

Panax spp.
(Wonder of the World)

LOVE, PROSPERITY, LONG LIFE

GOOD HEALTH

Make a wish

Cast it to the winds

Use this herb for any magickal

workings where the desired outcome

is one of the above, Ginseng will attract

Goldenbough

Viscum spp., Phoradendron
(Mistletoe)

FINANCIAL PROSPERITY

Carry with you in a green mojo bag

to attract money

Add a gold coin to the bag

and place on the cash register

of your business

Grains of Paradise

Amomum Granum-paradisi, A. Melegueta (Guinea Grains)

PASSION

JOY IN THE HOME

Add to spells where you need to
turn up the heat and make it sizzle

Sprinkle over a red Rose
and light a wishing candle

Make a herbal amulet to hang in the
home to usher in happiness and joy

Guinea Pepper

(Cayenne Pepper)

PROSPERITY AND SPEED

Add a pinch to all magickal workings
that require a speedy result
This herb is often used in Voodoo
and Santeria

Great when added to a spell
pouch or mojo bag
to attract prosperity

Gum Arabic

Acacia Nilotica, Senegalia (Acacia) Senegal, Achellia (Acacia) Seyal (Acacia Gum)

PSYCHIC POWER

CONTACT OTHER PLANES

Normally used as a bonding agent
for incense

Burn to develop your psychic talents
or before a séance to clear the
pathways and help to part the veil

*H*awthorn
Crateagus Oxycanthus

FAERY BLESSINGS

LOVE AND LUCK

Hawthorn is sacred to the Goddess

and is usually burned at Beltane

or given as an offering

One of the triad sacred to

The Fey (Faery Folk) along with

Oak and Ash

Hawthorn will attract love and luck

and ground you to Mother Earth

Carry or burn as an incense

Place on the altar at Beltane

$\mathcal{H}$eartsease

Viola Tricolor
(Johnny Jump-Up)

COMFORT AND ROMANCE

Just as the name suggests
Heartsease will bring comfort
and ease to a heart in pain
and will attract romance into your life

These spriggy little flowers
should be cut and placed in a vase
in the family room where they
will exude their magick to all
or carried in a spell pouch

*H*emlock Leaves

Tsuga spp.

To bind someone from doing harm
place the herb in a paper bag
upon which you have written their name
then bind the bag nine times
around with black cord
Tie and bury

Carry in a white mojo bag
to deflect bad vibes or hexes

*H*ibiscus

Hibiscus Sabdariffa

CLAIRVOYANCE, PSYCHIC ABILITY,
DIVINATION

Use the flowers as decoration in the home
to usher in a vibe of peace and tranquillity

Use the petals in spell crafting

Place the flowers around the altar
or work space, when you are ready to begin
divination or any work on the astral plane.

*H*igh John The Conqueror

Ipomea Jalapa

SUCCESS AND GOOD FORTUNE

Especially for artists and people in business

Carry with you

and have some in your work area

to build successful ventures

High John The Conqueror

is said to ward off depression

and negativity that many artistic

and creative people deal with

$\mathcal{H}$oneysuckle

Lonicera spp.

THIRD EYE, ASTRAL TRAVEL, PROSPERITY

Burn as an incense to open the third eye
and to develop an understanding of
astral images

Float flowers in a water bowl
with 3 gold coins
and a floating green candle
to usher prosperity into the home

Hoodwort

Scutellaria Lateriflora
(*See also Skullcap)

CONSECRATION AND FAITHFULNESS

Use at any event or time where
commitments and vows are made
Sprinkle on parchment to seal the magick
and bind the oath

Place under the head of the bed
to keep a partner faithful and true

Can be added to a spell pouch
to help someone see your
point of view

$\mathcal{H}$ops

Humulus Lupulus
(Beerbud)

HEALING SLEEP

Dried Hops are great for sleep pillows

which should be placed beneath

your regular night time pillow

so that the aroma wafts gently

rather than overcomes

Although not the most enjoyable aroma

if you combine the Hops with a little Lavender

it should help towards a

restful night's sleep

Horehound

Marrubium Vulgare

BLESSINGS RITUALS

FOCUS AND PROTECTION

Bless the home by placing
above the mantle

Sacred to the Egyptian God Horus
Burn as an incense to intensify
your ability to focus your thoughts

Horehound is protective during rituals

*H*yssop
Hyssopus Officinalis

PURIFY AND CLEANSE

Add to bathwater and soak
before ceremonies

Infuse in a cup of hot water
then sprinkle on magickal tools
and around magickal places
like altars, cauldrons and work spaces

Areas used as permanent circles
are always in need of extra care
and should be purified and cleansed
on a regular basis

Irish Moss

Chondrus Crispus
(Carrageen Moss)

POWER OF THE MOON,
WATER AND RAIN

Add to any spell crafting

that involves water

Particularly powerful if added

to your workings when outside

during the full moon

Jasmine Flowers
Jasminum spp.

AURA STRENGTHENER
BOOSTS CREATIVITY
ASTRAL TRAVEL

The smoke of the Jasmine Flower
should be smudged around
the body to give the aura
strength and energy
Particularly good after illness
as it works to strengthen you from
the astral plane into the physical plane

Burn Jasmine incense whenever
you need to be creative
it will heighten your abilities

Job's Tears
Coix Lacryma

MAGICKAL WISHES AND DREAMS

PROSPERITY

Create a magickal wish necklace

by threading the tears

Add other beads in between to represent

different magickal moments in your life

When not wearing you can carry

the necklace like a charm in a velvet bag

as a constant reminder to you

to live a magickal life!

Carry in a mojo bag to call forth

prosperity

$\mathcal{J}$oe Pye Weed
Eutrochium spp.

ATTRACT LOVE AND RESPECT

GAIN FAVOUR WITH THOSE

IN HIGH PLACES

Add to all magickal workings
where love is the desired outcome

Carry in a blue sachet or pouch
closely on your person
to garner respect and favour
from those around you

Particularly good for the individual in
a high powered work situation

Juniper Berries
Juniperus spp.

FOIL A THIEF

STAY SAFE

Place the herb near a door in the
home to deter theft

Carry with you to stay safe

Add to spells for good health
and well being to give them a boost

Juniper Berries are known
to be great curse and hex breakers
Add to pouches or burn as incense

*K*notgrass

Polygonum spp.
(Smartweed)

BIND YOUR WORRIES

Write down whatever is worrying you

Then place your note inside an envelope

add some of the herb to the envelope

then roll it up and

bind with a black cord

that you have tied thrice around

Breathe deeply each time you

wind the cord

Once to bind

Twice to relax

Three times to let go

Lady's Mantle
Alchemilla Vulgaris

TO MANIFEST AND FOCUS
RITUALS TO MOTHER EARTH OR GODDESS

Use outdoors during rituals
to harness the power of the earth
and focus your thoughts
as you repeat 3 times
"By the Lady blessed be!"

Sprinkle within the circle during
full moon rituals
or burn as an incense while spell
crafting to focus your intent

*L*avender
Lavandula spp.
(Elf Leaf)

ASTRAL VISION
PURIFICATION, SLEEP AND HEALING

Burn as an incense to aid astral travel
Lavender will help open the third eye and
permit visions of other worldly beings

Use in baths and washes to purify
and assist in healing

Add to sleep pillows
on its own or with Hops to help
you get a good night's rest

*L*emon Balm

Melissa Officinalis
(Melissa)

As a fragrance, Lemonbalm will perk up
your Chi life force and brighten your day

Carry to promote successful dealings with
others or add to other spell-craftings that
require a pinch of success

*L*emongrass

Cymbopogon Citratus

HONESTY AND FIDELITY

CLAIRVOYANCE AND DIVINATION

PSYCHIC ABILITY

COMMUNICATION WITH OTHER PLANES

Best burned as an incense
when endeavouring to contact the
higher planes or when honing
your psychic abilities

Place a sachet of the herb
near the bed to keep honesty
flowing in your relationship

Lemon Verbena

Aloysia Citrodora

CREATIVITY, POWER AND ATTRACTION

To enhance creativity
place in a dish
next to a person seeking an
artistic or musical epiphany
Let the aroma gently waft around them
and watch as their creativity begins to flow

Add to love spells, pouches and sachets
to boost their power of attraction

Licorice Root

Glycyrrhiza Glabra

LOVE AND FIDELITY

MARRIAGE

Place 2 pieces of Licorice Root into

a salver or cauldron

Add the petals of a Rose

and a sprig of Rosemary

Take a piece of parchment upon which

you have written the name of your beloved

Cut into confetti and add to the pot

Light a white candle

Add 2 drops of the wax into the mix

Sprinkle the mix outside to the North, South,

East and West as you make a wish for

your future together

Inside let the candle burn half way

then snuff and bind nine times around

with a white ribbon

Keep the bound candle somewhere in your

bedroom until your wish is granted

*L*ife *Everlasting*
Helichrysum Stoechas

GOOD HEALTH AND LONG LIFE

YOUTH AND BEAUTY

Place in a green mojo bag

and hang in the bathroom

near the mirror

to keep a youthful mind and heart

and as a reminder that

beauty does not belong only to the young

but shines from within

and can be found at all ages

Lily Flower
Lilium spp.

FERTILITY, RENEWAL AND SPRING

Burn as an incense for Ostara, the Spring Equinox
to remind you of new growth and the rebirth
of Mother Earth in the Spring

Make a fertility charm by adding
the Lily Flower to a handful of Clover
which grows in abundance
one spoonful of Mother Earth
and a pinch of Ginger powder to speed
things along

*L*inden Flower

Tilia spp.
(Lime Flower)

DISPELS NEGATIVE VIBES

Best when left in an open jar
or bowl within the magickal household
so that the flowers can vibrate
and lift the energy of the room

Lobelia

Lobelia spp.
(Indian Tobacco)

POWER OF THE FOUR WINDS

BREATHE

Powder the herb and cast
in the direction of an oncoming storm
to alter its course

Gather the flowers to sprinkle over
letters and parcels going overseas
to ensure a safe and speedy delivery

Lotus Root

Nymphaea Lotus

LOVE RITUALS

CALL FORTH A SPIRIT

Burn as an incense during a séance
to help clear the way for a Spirit to enter
or when evoking or invoking

Chop into pieces and add to a pink velvet
or satin pouch along with your
other love charms

Lotus Root will add power to the spell,
charm or mojo bag

Lovage Root

Levisticum Officinale
(Loveroot or Sea Parsley)

ATTRACTION

Add to bath water and soak
to become more attractive to others

Sprinkle chopped root over love letters
before you send them to attract a lover

*L*ucky Hand Root
Orchis spp.
(Salep Orchid)

SUCCESS AND GOOD FORTUNE

Should be worn in the correct spot
for maximum success

Place in the purse to attract money

In the shoes for safe travel

or sporting events

In your hat to improve brain power

Near the heart for matters of love

In your briefcase for success at work

Maidenhair Fern

Adiantum Capillus

PEACE, HARMONY AND TRANQUILITY

APHRODISIAC

Hang the fern close to the front
or back door of your home to usher in
peace and harmony
Or in a specific room to make a
tranquil area

Add pieces of the fern to aphrodisiac
charms and spells

Mandrake Root
Mandragora Officinalis

STRONG MAGICKAL POWER

Add to any spell or mojo bag to increase
its power

This age old magickal favourite can be
added to incense or charms
indeed any magickal workings
will be enhanced by the inclusion
of this root

Use the root to bind another by
wrapping it in some parchment upon which
you have written their name
then bury in the garden

Marshmallow Root
Althaea Officinalis
(Althea)

LOVE AND PROTECTION
REACH OTHER PLANES OF EXISTENCE

Carry with you for love and protection
in a purple pouch or mojo bag

Burn as an incense or scatter
around the area you intend to
use for contacting other realms

Can be added to protective pouches
that are to be hung in the home

Meadowsweet
Filipendula Ulmaria

HANDFASTINGS AND WEDDINGS

LOVE, PEACE AND JOY

Add to confetti at Handfastings or
Weddings to increase joy at the occasion
and to usher in a sense of peace

Meadowsweet can be added to all
Love pouches and spells

To recapture that feeling of
first being in love,
sprinkle over a wedding photo
and under the bed

Mugwort

Artemisia Vulgaris

PROPHETIC DREAMS

MANIFESTATION

PSYCHIC ABILITY

Burn as an incense before going to bed
to increase the likelihood of prophetic dreams

Excellent herb to aid you in expanding
your psychic abilities

To manifest that which you desire,
place the herb in an orange mojo bag
next to a representation of what you require

It is said that if you place a little in your
shoes it will ward off fatigue

Mullein

Verbascum Thapsus
(Graveyard Dust)

SAID TO WARD OFF DEMONS

GIVES COURAGE

Here is one from my Nanna's day

Carry with you in a yellow mojo bag
to lend you an aura of courage

An overpowering detriment to demons
and evil spirits
Draw a pentacle and sprinkle the
dust around it as you chant
the required spell

These days you can add a pinch
to any spell crafting or pouches to
increase courage and ward off bad vibes

*M*yrrh

Commiphora Myrrha

**BLESSINGS AND CONSECRATION
OF RITUALS AND TOOLS**

MYRRH FOR MAGICK!

**AN EXCELLENT ALL ROUND HERB
TO BURN AS AN INCENSE DURING RITUALS**

Myrrh increases magickal workings

and should be used for consecrating all

tools of the craft, like the Athame and Wand

by passing them through the smoke

Nutmeg
(Myristica Fragrans)

PROTECTION WITHIN THE CIRCLE

FERTILITY

DIVINATION

Grind into a powder to sprinkle around
the circle for protection

Use the whole Nutmeg in spell pouches
and mojo bags for fertility

Burn as an incense to enhance
divination abilities

Oakmoss

Evernia Prunastri

POWER OF THE EARTH

POWER OF ATTRACTION

Males should carry Oakmoss
in a pouch or sachet to attract a female

Can be used as a representation of the
element Earth during rituals

With its power to attract,
add Oakmoss to green mojo bags
filled with other prosperity ingredients

O_{ak}

Quercus spp.

On a Thursday

Gather sticks from the Oak tree and bind

them together with a blue ribbon or cord

Place the sticks outside near the

doorway to your home for their

protective qualities

Use an Oak branch for wand making

Its qualities of strength and stability

will serve you well when spell crafting

Orange Peel
Citrus Sinensis

LOVE AND MARRIAGE

PROSPERITY AND GOOD FORTUNE

Best used for formulas whose
intent is to take you from
love to marriage

Sprinkle the zest
over a bouquet of flowers
then take them into the garden
and throw them over your right shoulder
Walk away without looking back

Use in sachets and potions
For prosperity and good fortune

Orris Root

Iris Pallida
(Queen Elizabeth Root)

LOVE AND STICKING POWER

The Powder of the Orris Root has
long been used as a fixative in
things like potpourri as it
allows a fragrance to last longer

In spellcrafting the Orris Root
should be added for love and longevity
and to make a spell 'stick'

*P*assionflower

Passiflora Incarnata

ALLAY WORRIES

HELP SLEEP

FIND A FRIEND

Write out your desire to find
a friend on a piece of parchment
Roll up and place in a white mojo bag
along with the Passionflower
carry with you

Place in an open dish
in the bedroom
to calm the mind and help sleep

*P*atchouli Leaves
Pogostemon Cablin

ATTRACTION AND LOVE

USE BY THE MALE TO ATTRACT A FEMALE

Carry with you in a pouch

to which you should add some Rose petals

and Oakmoss

Add to a potpourri mix

When placed in the correct spot

it will gently waft its magick

throughout the area

Pennyroyal

Mentha Pulegium
(Squaw Mint)

PROTECT AND INVIGORATE

Place a small pad with a touch of
Pennyroyal in your shoe
To give you a boost during the day

Burn as an incense when casting
protection spells

Pennyroyal is great for your dog's bedding
A natural flea deterrent and repellent
Place a little inside your friends bedding

*P*eony Flowers
Paeonia spp.

GUARDS THE HOME
STRENGTHENS THE ETHERIC BEING

Wear or carry the flowers for personal
protection and to strengthen the aura
from those who would suck the life
out of it during the day!

Place in the home
to ward off all manner of evils
Peony Flowers were used in part
to keep away incubi and succubi

*P*eppermint

Mentha Piperita

CLEANSING AND HEALING

MIND CLEARING

Add to healing potions and sachets

Burn as an incense in the home
to help keep away colds and flu
Peppermint is also an excellent
cleansing agent

Add a little of the fragrance
to a tissue
when inhaled during the day it will
keep you from feeling drowsy

Periwinkle
Vinca Minor
(Sorcerer's Violet)

REGAIN A LOST MEMORY

POWER

LEARN TO LOVE YOURSELF

It is said that if you stare at the
herb it will bring back a
memory long lost

Soak the herb in a cup of hot
water, when cool wash over
all the mirrors in the house
so that when you gaze upon yourself
you will learn to love what you see

Periwinkle can be added to all spells
to give an added power boost

*P*oke Root

Phytolacca Americana

TO FIND WHAT WAS LOST
TO GIVE COURAGE

Carry with you in a yellow
mojo bag or pouch when you need
an extra boost of courage

Take the root along with a sprig
of Rosemary to remember
and a little Mugwort for manifestation
and leave in the room you last saw
the missing item

*P*oppy Seeds
Papaver Somniferum
(Khaskhas)

Carry the seeds on your person

for fertility

They can also be added to love

charms and spells where required

To attract money make a ring of

Poppy Seeds around a green candle

Burn on a new or waxing moon

Rattlesnake Root
Nabalus Albus

POWER TO OVERCOME

Overcome obstacles or negative vibes
by carrying in an orange mojo bag
with a piece of Amber and a
pinch of Ginger

For students, place the mojo bag
inside the desk where you study

Rosemary
Rosmarinus Officinalis

TO REMEMBER

PROTECTION FOR THOSE WHO TRAVEL
OVER THE WATER

Plant Rosemary by the garden gate

my mother used to say

Add to all magickal workings where you

need to keep a memory alive

For travellers

Make a tea and wash the outside of your

suitcase with the mixture

For personal protection add to bath

water and soak before your journey

Rose of Jericho
Anastatica Hierochuntina
(Resurrection Herb)

MULTIPLE BLESSINGS!

Add to water and the Jericho Rose

will come to life

Place in the home for abundant blessings

Keep adding water to the dish or bowl

and once a week sprinkle some of

the water at the front door

to usher in peace and happiness

Roses
Rosa spp.

LOVE AND PASSION

COURAGE, PURITY AND CALM

ADD TO CONFETTI

Use the Rose buds, full blooms or petals

The colour will depend on the

spell or charm

Generally Pink for love

Red for passion

White for purity and protection

Yellow for courage and to

ward off negativity

Lilac to calm and centre

Add to homemade confetti

for Weddings and Handfastings

$\mathcal{R}ue$

Ruta Graveolens
(Herb of Grace)

Rue can be added to spell-craftings
to complete them and give an
extra boost of power

Add to health and wellbeing sachets
or mojo bags to help ward off
all manner of illness

*S*afflower

Carthamus Tinctorius

Can be substituted where a recipe calls

for Saffron which can be

very expensive

Burn as an incense to expand psychic

abilities or add to mojo bags for

Love and prosperity

Sage
Salvia Officinalis

WISDOM AND LONGEVITY

CLEANSING AND CLEARING

Great burnt as a smudge to clear and
cleanse your magickal areas

Carry with you to promote wisdom

Add to herbal health sachets to
infuse longevity into the mix

*S*aint John's Wort
Hypericum Perforatum

POWER TO RULE

STRENGTH AND CONFIDENCE

PROTECTS AGAINST
FIRE, LIGHTNING AND EVIL SPIRITS

Carry with you to gain confidence

and strengthen your resolve

Saint John's Wort is said to give one

the ability to take charge of situations

Put in a glass jar with lid

Draw a pentacle on the lid then

place near doors and windows to

protect the house from fire, lightning

and evil spirits

Sandalwood

Santalum Album, Santalum Spicatum

Sandalwood is highly vibrational

It acts upon both the physical and etheric

bodies to protect

Burn as an incense in magickal spaces

altars and work areas

particularly before any psychic

or clairvoyant work is undertaken

Sacred to the Angel Sandalphon

Burn before evoking

*S*arsaparilla

Smilax Regelii, Smilax Ornata

KEEP A SECRET

APHRODISIAC

Having trouble keeping a secret?

Write 'I will never tell' on parchment

add Sarsaparilla

fold into a small square and tie

with a black ribbon

Find a body of water like a

stream, lake or ocean

Face away from the water and throw

the parchment over your left shoulder

into the water

Walk away without looking back

You will never tell!

Add to passion potions and love sachets

where appropriate

Skullcap
(*See also Hoodwort)

USE FOR VOWS AND COMMITTMENTS

TO BIND AND CONSECRATE

To stay True to Your Love

place under the bed

Use at Weddings and Handfastings

for Official Documents

and over Handfasting ties

*S*ea Spirit

Gelidium Amansii, Gelidium Corneum
(Agar Agar)

Make an infusion with hot water

when cool sprinkle around

the home to bring new

opportunities and blessings

Make a wash from the infusion

for suitcases before travelling

over water

Call to the Spirits of the Sea

ask for their protection and blessings

upon your journey

Self-Heal
Prunella Vulgaris
(Healall)

Add an infusion to a bath

and soak in it for personal

self healing

Sprinkle in sick rooms

to lift the vibration and begin the

healing process

*S*enna Leaves

Senna Alexandrina, Senna spp.

CO-OPERATION AND DIPLOMACY

BUSINESS DEALINGS

TACT

Take a mojo bag to work with you
filled with Senna Leaves
and place in the desk drawer
to help business deals run smoothly

Use in spellcrafting where
a certain amount of tact and diplomacy
are necessary to reach a
suitable conclusion

*S*esame Seeds

Sesamum Indicum

INCREASE YOUR MONEY

Sprinkle the Sesame Seeds in money pouches

to increase cash flow

Add a pinch of Ginger to speed the process

Place a ring of Sesame Seeds

around a green candle

and burn on a Thursday during

the waxing moon

Slippery Elm
Ulmus Rubra

Add to spells that require a release
emotional or physical

To put an end to gossip or someone
speaking badly of you
write their name on a piece of
parchment then shake the
powder over it
Roll up the parchment like a scroll
and bind around with cord from
one end to the other
while you say three times
"I bind you from speaking badly of me
or of others"
Then burn the scroll (safely!)

*S*olomon's Seal
Polygonatum Biflorum

WISDOM AND KNOWLEDGE

INSPIRATION

Great to carry in a mojo bag

Blue for wisdom and knowledge

Purple for inspiration

Burn as an incense before major

decisions or exams

or for artists and musicians

burn to inspire

Southernwood

Artemisia Abrotanum
(Lad's Love)

LOVE AND DESIRE

Soak in a bath before a Wedding
or Handfasting

Add to love spells, pouches, sachets or
mojo bags to carry with you

*S*peedwell
Veronica spp.

RAPID RECOVERY AFTER ILLNESS

Just as the name suggests

place Speedwell in sick rooms to

speed up the recovery process

You can make a herbal bath

and soak in it

or add to spell crafting

*S*pikenard

Nardostachys Jatamansi

ANIMAL TRAINING

FOCUS AND UNDERSTANDING

FAITHFULNESS AND ATTRACTION

Best used as an incense

It will open the channels of
communication when training
an animal

Clear the mind and
give focus and understanding when
undertaking study of any kind

Helps attract a new love
and keep them faithful

*S*purge
Euphorbia spp.

REPELS NEGATIVITY

PROTECTS

REMOVES A CURSE OR HEX

Carry with you in a purple
pouch or mojo bag
This age old magickal herb is known
for its ability to protect from even
the most negative of energies

To remove a hex
simply place some of the herb in
an envelope that you have addressed
'return to sender'
Draw a stamp on the front
and bury in the garden
Sprinkle Skullcap (Hoodwort) on top
to "fix" the spell

*S*tar Anise
Illicium Verum

Place the Star Anise on a mantle
to usher in good luck for the home

You can carry with you for personal luck
or add to mojo bags where an
extra boost of luck is required

Tansy
Tanacetum Vulgare

LONG LIFE AND LONG LOVE

Place the herb on a blue paper
then fold into a square
Draw a Star of David
or six pointed star on the outside
and tie with a blue ribbon or cord
Light a blue candle
and drip some of the wax into the centre of
the star to "bind" the spell

This can be carried with you or placed
in a special spot in your home

*T*hyme
Thymus Vulgaris

Thyme is excellent for healing past
sorrows as it brings them to the top
and then begins the healing process

Burn as an incense before study
to stimulate the mind and memory
and to cleanse magickal areas
before any rituals

Add to healing mojo bags

Tonka Beans

Dipteryx Odorata

MAGICKAL WISHING BEANS

Make a wish as you hold the bean in the
palm of your left (incoming) hand
then throw the bean over your right
shoulder into the garden

Take four beans

place them in a pouch

One for good health

Two for luck

Three for happiness

Four for prosperity

Add a Lucky Hand Root and some

Mandrake Root for a very

powerful magickal charm

$\mathcal{U}$nicorn Root

Aletris Farniosa
(True Unicorn Root)

SENSUALITY

REMOVES HEX'S AND CROSSINGS

TO KEEP A GHOST AT BAY

This very rare herb can be used in
spells and charms to enhance
one's sensuality

Carry with you in a black mojo
bag to absorb all manner
of negative energies

Ghostly activity will cease when you
place this herb in a room
so will any poltergeist and spirit problems

Valerian

Valeriana Officinalis

HIGHLY PURIFYING

HEAL A RIFT

STOP A QUARREL

Chop the root and add to a mojo bag

along with some Maidenhair Fern

and Passionflower

leave the bag in the room where

a quarrel is taking place

to calm the situation

purify the air and heal the rift

Vanilla Bean Pod
Vanilla Planifolia

ENERGIZING

ATTRACT LOVE

Use the Vanilla Bean pod in
potpourri as it will energize the area
that it is placed in

To attract love it should be carried
as part of a love charm

Vervain

Verbena Hastata

INSPIRATION FOR ARTISTS

SINGERS AND POETS

SUCCESS

SPIRITUAL ENERGIES

USE TO CONSECRATE ARTIST'S TOOLS
AND MAGICKAL TOOLS

It is said that Vervain will attract

only the highest spiritual energy

and bring personal satisfaction and success

For inspiration place some where you

practice your craft

*V*etivert

Vetiveria Zizanioides
(Khuskhus)

Use the powder to add to spells

and mojo bags

or burn as an incense

Vetivert will increase the power

of your spellcrafting

*V*iolet

Viola Odorata

USE THE FLOWER OR THE LEAF

ASSOCIATED WITH VENUS AND LOVE

Best time to gather is at twilight or dawn
for the most power

Add to love spells and sachets along
with Rose and Lavender for a powerful
and highly vibrational blend

If you are having a string of bad luck
Violet can be carried with you
to transform and attract a change

White Oak Bark

Quercus Alba
(King Oak)

Usually comes in a powder
which you can burn on a charcoal block
before attempting to access other worlds

The White Oak Bark powder offers
protection, endurance and strength on
the journey whilst acting as
a conduit and linking the realms

White Sage

Salvia Apiana

CLEANSING AND PURIFYING

SACRED TO NATIVE AMERICANS

Used mostly as a smudge by binding
the Sage branches together
with wool or cotton

Smudging is great for large areas
that need cleansing quickly

Can also be burned as an incense
in a room with the same effect

Willow

Salix spp.

POWER OF THE MOON

WAND MAKING

HEALING

SPIRIT COMMUNICATION

Use the bark of the tree or the branch
if wand making
Willow is the lightest and most magickal
of trees to work with and is powered by
the full moon

Add the bark to healing spells
or make into a powder for sachets

Will help open the doorway between worlds
when used on the waning moon
to contact a spirit

*W*olfsbane

Aconitum Napellus
(Monkshood)

*TOXIC!
EXTREME CAUTION SHOULD BE USED
AS EVEN HANDLING THIS HERB
CAN CAUSE ACCIDENTAL POISONING

PROTECTION

HEX BREAKER

Use in house and home,

protection spells and mojo bags

Make a mojo bag

and hang above the front door

Witch Hazel

Hamamelis Virginiana
(Spotted Alder)

DISPERSE NEGATIVE ENERGY

HELP HEAL A BROKEN HEART

Leave in the home to disperse
negative energies as they enter

Carry in a pink mojo bag
with some Heartsease
to help heal a broken heart

Woodruff

Galium Odoratum
(Master of the Woods)

SUCCESS AND VICTORY

CHANGE YOUR WAYS

Burn before games, matches
or events where you would like to
have a positive outcome

Change your ways for the better
by carrying in a red mojo bag or pouch

Wood Rose

Rosa Gymnocarpa

ATTRACTION

POWER AND BLESSINGS

Used greatly in Voodoo
for its ability to bring power
and blessings to the user

Sprinkle over the Altar
before Sabats and Esbats

Use in spell crafting to attract
love, money or success by scribing
your desire on a piece
of parchment to wrap around
the Wood Rose, tie with a pink ribbon
for love, green for money and
blue for success
Leave on the mantle for three days

Wormwood

Artemesia Absinthium
(Absinthe)

VISIONS IN THE NIGHT

CONTACT WITH SPIRITS

SLOW AN ENEMY

Wormwood is one of the herbs

often called a 'Witch herb'

Used by both solitaires and covens

in rituals to call forth spirits

or to have night visions

Add to your spells

to slow down an enemy's progress

but never to harm

$\mathcal{Y}$*arrow*

Achillea Millefolium

THE WITCH'S HERB

COURAGE

FRIENDSHIP AND LOVE

Add to herbal pouches and mojo bags
for friendship and love spells

For courage aplenty
hold the Yarrow in your power hand
it is said to allay all fear

Attach above the bedhead
to ensure lasting love of seven
years or more

Yellow Dock Root

Rumex Crispus

MONEY AND PROSPERITY

A very strong attractor of money
and continuous prosperity
My purse has never been empty!

Add the Yellow Dock Root to a
green pouch or mojo bag and add
a piece of Citrine crystal
Citrine is also well known for its
ability to attract money

Carry with you near your wallet
or place in a cash register
next to the gold coins

Spells

❖ *Amulet of Release* ❖

❖ *Prosperity Spell* ❖

❖ *Safe Travel* ❖

❖ *Protect the Home* ❖

❖ *Locate a Lost Item* ❖

❖ *House Clearing Salts* ❖

❖ *Love Spell* ❖

❖ *Tincture of Gold* ❖

*A*mulet of Release

A

AB

ABRA

ABRAC

ABRACA

ABRACAD

ABRACADA

ABRACADAB

ABRACADABR

ABRACADABRA

The Abracadabra, a favourite of children and stage magicians is in fact an ancient Celtic amulet some thousands of years old. Abra meaning God and Cad meaning holy

It should be written starting with the full word and losing one letter as you go, finally ending with the letter 'A' in Hebrew aleph, the beginning.

The Abracadabra was a powerful amulet for removing illness and worry and is probably based on one even older – the abhadda kedabhra meaning disappear like this word from the ancient Aramaic language.

Finish with the 'A' at the top for matters of the heart and healing.

Finish with the 'A' at the bottom for more earthly problems

Like finance, work or worldly worries.

Prosperity Spell

On a Thursday

Place 3 gold coins in a mojo bag or pouch

Add some Sesame Seeds

and a piece of Citrine

Light a green candle

hold the pouch

"Prosperity draw near to me

luck and money and winnings be

mine to have and mine to see

I charge these coins come back to me

many fold – So mote it be"

Carry the coins for three days

then send them out into the world

Safe Travel

Soak the herbs Comfrey and Burdock Root

add some water and make a wash

for the outside of your suitcase

Light a blue candle

and say:

"Universal forces be

safe and true surrounding me

wherever I stay, wherever I go

my way is clear

I will it so!"

*P*rotect the Home

Take four nails, hold them in your left hand and say:

"I create a barrier around this door
trouble and strife will enter no more
I charge these nails to keep me safe"

Now hammer them into the four corners of the
lintel around your door

For windows charge three nails
and hammer them in a pyramid shape
to form a barrier keeping evil out
It is wise to hang a pentagram down the
left hand side of the window, whenever we moved
to a new house, which was a lot,
the first thing we did
was to hang the pentagram on the window
and place the Mezuzah's on the doors
It always made me feel safe and protected

Locate a Lost Item

In the room where you last saw the item

light a white candle

and circle it with Thyme to stimulate

your memory

Say out Loud

"What I seek is lost to me

cosmic forces set it free

bring it back to ease my pain

to come and dwell with me again"

Then say three times

"Wherever Ye be

Come to me"

Most items will return within a few days

However, some have been gifted

to another by the universe for a specific purpose

and may never return to you

*H*ouse Clearing Salts

Nothing better for nasty built up energies

Particularly good if you are moving
to a new home to remove any negative vibrations
or if a lot of arguments have taken place
where you live

Half fill a glass jar with natural sea salt
To this add the herbs
Sage and Yarrow
Clap the hands or ring a bell
in each room
Light a black candle to absorb as you go
Shake and sprinkle a little of the salt
Don't forget the corners
After one hour open the windows
and sweep the rooms clear
Snuff out the candle
and play some loud upbeat music

Love Spell

Gather the petals of a red or pink Rose
and the seeds from the heart of a red Apple
Place them in a mortar and pound with the pestle

In a small glass jar, place a Rose Quartz
crystal or tumble stone
Half fill the jar with Almond oil
to this add 3 drops of Amber oil

Mix in the Rose petals and Apple seeds
place the lid on and
let it stand until the full moon

Place a little on the wrist five minutes before

you speak with your beloved and make

sure you touch their arm at least once

as you speak to them.

This spell works on an ethereal level

quietly and delicately.

Of course no one can make another person

fall in love with them

if there is nothing there to begin with

but for those who just need a little push

in the right direction,

this is just the thing.

*T*incture *of* Gold

INCREASES MAGICKAL ENERGY
BY THE POWER OF THREE

IS NOT TO BE CONSUMED
AND SHOULD BE USED SPARINGLY

Gold is the highest conductor

of magickal energy there is.

Simply place a dot of the tincture

on any item you wish to

channel energy through or to.

On the night of a full moon gather:

one cup of water from a natural source

one piece of plain gold or broken gold jewellery

Rainwater gathered during a storm

is particularly powerful.

Find a piece of broken gold jewellery, 9ct at least,

a ring or a pendant work well.

This must be heated and plunged

into the pure water

three times to supercharge the water molecules

with the gold. Use pliers to hold the jewellery

Take care not to burn yourself as the water will sizzle

Pour the charged water into a small bottle and seal

then draw a pentagram on the label

and leave out under the full moon until the sun rises

as gold is charged by the sun

Craftings and More

⁕ How to Make a Powerful Wand ⁕

Traditional Tree Types

Instructions for Making Your Wand

Best Crystals for Wand Making

⁕ Keeping and Decorating a Book of Shadows ⁕

What Should You Find in a Book of Shadows?

Now for Making Your Book Look Fabulous!

⁕ Bringing Nature Spirits to Your Garden ⁕

Creating a Faery Circle

How to See Faeries

⁕ The Aura ⁕

Colours in the Aura

$\mathcal{H}$ow to Make a Powerful Wand

The wand is one of our main magickal implements. It is used to direct energy and to draw magickal symbols on the earth. If you do not have an Athame, the wand can be used instead to cast circle. It can also be used as a healing tool as it will direct positive energies and vibrations from you into anything you desire; people, pets, plants etc.

Wands come in all types – everyday 'working' wands, crystal tipped wands for Sabbats and special occasions and double ended crystal healing wands to name but a few. They are made from a variety of substances relating to their use and the personal preference of the crafter, but for my money, the most powerful wands are those made by hand from one of the traditional magickal woods – Oak, Elder, Ash, Hawthorn, Hazel, Holly or my particular favourite, Willow. It has a wonderful, magickal quality to it and is as light as a feather to work with and very easy to carve.

If you are reticent about trying to make your own wand, don't be. You will find that not only is it an easy task, it's also one of the most enjoyable crafts to undertake; the real work lies in the preparation. If you stick to it, you will create for yourself a fine, hand crafted wand that will last a lifetime and gain in power through the years.

To begin with, you must find a stick or branch of wood. Traditionally the length should be from your elbow to somewhere between the wrist and the tip of the index finger. The width should be anything from 15mm to 25mm in diameter. Obviously a wider branch will be easier to attach a crystal to.

The branch may present itself to you on the side of the road as you walk along or you could take yourself to a park (always a good spot to find a Willow tree).

If you must cut the branch from the tree, make sure it is done on the waning moon. Tell the tree of your intention to make a wand from its branch and give it time to withdraw its energy before you cut. If you can, cover the cut with some mud to aid in healing, then thank the tree for its contribution.

Traditional Tree Types

AND THEIR MAGICKAL ATTRIBUTES

Oak   Strength, courage, balance,
                 power and protection
                 for elemental spirits

Elder   For wisdom, to give thanks
                 and for Faery blessings

Ash   Associated with the Elves,
                 magickal awakenings and knowledge

Willow   Power of the Moon,
                 intuition and psychic ability

Hawthorn   Sacred to the Sidhe (Faery Folk)
                 Protection

Hazel   Brings transformation and creativity
                 Releases negative energies
                 Witchcraft

Holly   Enhances magickal abilities
                 Brings balance

Instructions for Making Your Wand

- 1 small sharp knife or hobby tool for stripping the bark
- 1 sheet of fine sandpaper
- Wood stain
- Beeswax polish

OPTIONAL EXTRAS

- A small crystal point
- Feathers
- A length of black cord or leather
- A piece of velvet material in your preferred colour

Start by trimming off any side twigs. I have always chosen wood that has a gnarl or two and sometimes even a bit of a bend. I find it makes for a much more interesting wand. Now take your time and carefully shave off the outer bark. Try to leave a layer of bark around the wand as this will polish up nicely later on. Don't worry if you can't, that's what the wood stain is for. If you have chosen a wood that it not fully dry, you may have to leave it for a week to dry out before you continue.

Once the outer layer of bark has been removed, use your sandpaper to give it a light sanding. Now pass the wand through the smoke of your favourite myrrh incense to cleanse and infuse with magick. If you have a particular tradition that you follow, it is at this point that you might like to give thanks or ask for guidance and blessings to help you use your wand to its best advantage. Finally, either stain or if you left a layer of bark, simply polish with the natural beeswax.

For decoration on your new wand, sew a small piece of velvet around the thickest end to act as a handle and bind with black cord or leather strap. Some like a handle, some don't. I fashion a handle tightly around the end of the wand out of dark brown clay that hardens by air, not by oven. These clays are readily available from craft stores in every colour imaginable. The clay being a natural substance from the earth, permits the wand to breathe and the natural energies to come through. You might like to try your hand at carving a word or symbol into your wand.

My favourite wand is made from Willow, with a bit of a crook towards the end and my witch name carved into it in a slightly lopsided manner. This particular wand has been with me for some 30 odd years and has gathered an immense amount of power!

The most popular things to carve into your wand include:

- Your Witch name in runes
- A Pentagram
- Triquetra
- Name of the archangel Raphael
  (if your wand represents the element air)
- Or Michael
  (if it represents fire in your particular tradition)
- Symbol of your star sign
- 'Blessings' in whatever tradition you follow

If you intend to attach a crystal to one end or to both ends, then drill a hole and use a natural resin based glue to set it. Feathers can also be attached, simply tuck them under the velvet before you bind around with the leather or cord. For more power, bind the end of the wand with copper wire, or magnetise a string (like a violin string) by rubbing a magnet down its length and then bind around.

Your completed wand, being a natural wood, will both channel and store energy easily and should be placed under the next full moon to charge.

Care of the wand is simple. Use it often. Polish with beeswax once a year and let it charge occasionally under the moon.

Best Crystals for Wand Making

Clear Quartz   The healing crystal. Cleanses the mind and body of toxins. Contains all the colours of the spectrum as it reflects pure white light. Can vibrate the seven chakras simultaneously.

Amethyst   Protects and heals, aids psychic abilities. Great for meditation. Promotes sweet dreams. Guides the mind to wisdom.

Rose Quartz   Emanates calm, love and peace. Comforts and soothes the heart. Heals inner wounds.

Amber   Stabilizing, grounding, revitalizing. Amber's golden ray can help with depression

Lapis Lazuli   Stone of Power. Aids intuition, extra sensory perception and meditative ability. Cleanses the aura.

Carnelian   Focus. Protection. Good for meditation. Helps delve into the past and past lives.

Obsidian   Stone of truth.
                  Cleanses the mind and body.
                  Helps you to know yourself.

Citrine   Known for increasing wealth.
                  Helps focus and release anger
                  and increase intuition.

Ruby   Amplifies energy, stimulates the
                  mind. Protects and brings light to
                  the wearer. Helps access the higher
                  planes of existence.

Malachite   Channels higher energies.
                  All purpose healing stone
                  that absorbs rather than
                  emits vibrations.
                  Will draw out negative energies.
                  Protective.
                  Releases creative ability.

Moonstone   Calms and balances.
                  Stone for wishes and dreams.
                  Power of the moon.
                  Soothes the nerves.

Turquoise   Highly prized by American Indians
                  and Tibetan Shamans. Heals the
                  spirit and protects during vision
                  quests and astral travel. Aligns and
                  strengthens the chakras.

Agate Helps connect to the spiritual.
Balances.
Can help awaken latent talents.
Different colours of agate will bring
further qualities to the stone

Tiger's Eye Attunes the third eye.
Gives focus.
Enhances psychic ability,
releases fear and emanates
soothing vibrations.

Jade Prosperity and long life.
Promotes inner harmony.
Soothes the nervous system
and expels negative emotions
from the heart and soul.

Aquamarine Stone of courage.
Aligns the chakras.
Strengthens the aura.
Sharpens the intellect.
Helps to connect
with the higher self.

Keeping and Decorating a Book of Shadows

I remember well my grandmother's old, black Grimoire or Book of Secrets as she called it. From the outside it looked somewhat battered and plain, bulging at the seams with recipes and wisdoms that I had yet to learn, but inside the magick beamed from every page.

She would dry flowers and press them around the edge of the pages and write in a bold black script that looked as if it had been taken straight out of the 18th century.

Every recipe, potion and spell was lovingly recorded and each page was given something special; a cutting, a herb, a picture pasted in or a sketch drawn. For a page that she deemed of high importance my grandmother would drizzle a little candle wax and firmly press her ring into it, creating a magickal seal that further enhanced the power of those pages.

I know that many modern witches have lost the joy in keeping and decorating a Book of Shadows, some even going so far as to keep a computerised record instead! Well, I am a firm believer in each finding his or her own path, but for those who would like to try and infuse a little more interest in each page, here are a few ideas to get you started.

A Book of Shadows, unlike a Grimoire which is a magickal book that can be shared, is very personal to each individual and should be a recorded journey of your life as a witch. If you join a magickal coven the High Priestess may want to see your Book of Shadows to find out what magickal study you have been doing and to check on your progress so it's nice if you can add some interest to the pages.

I loved my Book of Shadows from the first moment it came to me and rather than finding all those empty pages daunting, I couldn't wait to fill them!

What Should You Find in a Book of Shadows?

- All things magickal pertaining to YOU! Keep a few pages for recording special magickal moments for instance initiation, hand fasting, naming ceremonies etc.
- Witch names.
- Recipes, spells and potions that you have made or tried.
- Chants, poems and witchy pictures of all kinds – Yes, you can stick pictures in it. A Book of Shadows should be hand written, but there's no law against adding extras to make it look good!
- Magickal charts/correspondences that you have pasted in to use as a reference or written in yourself for more power.
- Full Moon Chart for the year. (These must be changed every year of course)
- When you bought or made any magickal tools or implements.
- How you feel about your journey along the way.
- Things you have learned like:
- How to cast a circle
- Magickal alphabets (like the Witch's alphabet, ogham and runes)
- A section on herb lore and crystals.
- If your craft has taken you in a particular direction and you are specializing in one field more than the others then dedicate some pages to your passion.

Now for Making Your Book Look Fabulous!

PRESSED FLOWERS

I learned from experience just how good these look around a page. I also learned that they fade over time, but worry not! I found a way to have the best of both worlds.

First take yourself out into the garden, or a friend's garden if you don't have one, with a pair of scissors and a bowl. Most flowers are suitable for pressing, but the smaller ones are easier to work with. Try to leave some of the stem and maybe a leaf or two on for a more interesting look on your page.

Remember to thank each plant for its contribution to your magickal workings as you go.

Carefully place the flowers on a thick white serviette or paper towel and then place another over the top. You will need to put the serviettes inside the pages of a heavy book for about a week. The idea is to remove the moisture and flatten as soon as possible after cutting.

Once dry, place them around a page that's NOT part of your book. Attach with a little craft glue. Now take your page to a photocopying machine and run off as many copies as you need. They photocopy brilliantly and this way will never lose their colour and brilliance. Use the flowered pages as you will by attaching into your book of shadows as you go.

EASY WITCHY CALLIGRAPHY

Okay, so you think you have no drawing ability, well think again – witches have always been 'crafty' people. If you want your Book of Shadows or your written spells to look amazing, just follow these simple rules:

Always use a black pen, it's just so much more impressive and stick with one easy style; for instance every time you write a letter with a right 'leg' like A, m or n just add a hook to the leg beneath the line.

When you have a letter with a top 'arm' like k or h just hook them at the top. In fact the letters a, k and h can have a flourish both top and bottom. Take a little care as you go; after all, this is one book that will last you a lifetime. You might like to try a calligraphy pen. There's nothing like the look of real flowing ink on your pages.

MAGICKAL ALPHABETS

Make use of the Witch's alphabet, also known as
Theban or Angelic Script around the edge of the
pages like a border. You could use star signs or the
planetary symbols; not only does this look great, it
adds an extra touch of magick to your page.

Remember, you are trying to create interest and
add power.

A PERSONAL SEAL

For a different touch, light a purple candle and wait until some liquid has formed. Drizzle some wax in a small circle the size of a coin. Press a seal into the melted wax; use a piece of gold or silver jewellery like an ankh or a pentagram or you can buy a seal from a craft store. Remember to put some blotting paper underneath the page so that the wax doesn't go through to the next page. This seal can also be used on your written spells and to close your personal envelopes with a touch of magick.

A Modern Witch's Book of Shadows and Grimoire should be so filled with useful information and correspondences that you simply can't do without it. It should be scratched and dented from frequent use, with dog eared pages and bits and pieces sticking out of it, but most of all it should be loved to bits and added to on a regular basis.

Remember the more magick you put in, the more you get out!

$\mathcal{B}$ringing Nature Spirits to Your Garden

FAERIES ARE REAL – Faeries exist – and I'm not just talking about in our collective imaginations. They belong to the realm of Elementals and Nature Spirits that dwell in the lower subdivisions of the astral plane.

Their real names are Salamanders, Sylphs, Undines and Gnomes and they belong to the fire, air, water and earth realms respectively. There is a fifth elemental that belongs to the Ether and others that are as yet un-manifested.

We invoke them at our circle castings and rituals. They are as real as you and I. The job of these nature spirits is to work in their particular field of nature; building forms in the animal, vegetable and mineral realms. It is the nature spirits that guide the life force of plants and help build the compounds of crystals and minerals.

Nature spirits known in folklore as faeries, pixies, elves, water sprites and 'wee folk', have often been seen by the human eye because their vibratory level is very close to our own. It is a fact that we humans only use about 20 percent of the cones and rods in our eyes that help us to perceive light and colour.

Those who practice astral vision on a regular basis find that they slowly strengthen their eyes to a point where they are able to perceive the movement of these etheric creatures without too much bother.

Nowadays, due to the advent of digital cameras, many people are capturing orbs and strange light phenomenon, usually at twilight or just before dawn. Proof of the myriad of as yet unknown life forms that we share the ether with.

As a child I would daydream often about faeries at the bottom of my garden; flitting from flower to flower and sitting under a toadstool in the shade. Unfortunately these days, with the urban sprawl moving further and further out into the natural spaces, nature spirits have been pushed into the outer regions. They can however, still be found around natural pools and streams, in forests and wooded glades and sometimes, where the vibrations are sympathetic to their existence; in a back garden.

As my grandmother used to say:

"If you want the faery folk to come and stay,

you have to invite them!"

Creating a Faery Circle

To invite these wonderful creatures to come and dwell in your garden is a relatively simple process. Start by making a faerie circle out of rocks and stones. It doesn't have to be large, any size that fits a small area in your garden space will do. Elementals are attracted to the circular shape. Around the edge, plant some greenery. If you are in a rental property, potted greenery is fine and place a crystal in the middle of the circle.

Faery attractants include:

- Rosemary, Lavender, Hawthorn, Sunflower and Trefoil.
- For faery blessings, plant Elder
  But never plant Broom – faeries dislike it!
- Crystals that the faery kingdom are particularly fond of include: Fluorite, Jasper and Amethyst.

Make sure you use no poisons or unnatural substances in the faerie circle.

Now take a bowl of salted water, sea salt is best and sprinkle it inside the circle. On the night of the next full moon, perform this simple welcoming ritual.

THE WELCOMING

Light a white candle – Gather flower petals and
sprinkle them within the faery circle, then cast a
white light around it. Direct your good thoughts out
from the small circle to include your entire garden
and say:

"Trees and plants and flowers

be strong and tall for all to see

by the Sun and Moon at night

my garden is a sheer delight"

"Spirits of earth, air, fire, water

I welcome you to this Circle

and to this garden

in peace, love, joy and magick"

The etheric world is affected by our thoughts, words
and feelings, so the simple magick of vocalising your
request to the nature spirits will begin the process
immediately. You will notice a subtle change to the
atmosphere of your garden; a shift in the everyday
order of things. If you make it a regular practice to
send your good vibes and welcoming thoughts and
keep a magickal garden, then these wonderful spirits
of the elements will remain with you.

How to See Faeries

(THE ASTRAL LIGHT)

Anyone can learn to see faeries and sprites. Just find your ideal spot and make yourself comfortable then relax and let your gaze take you slowly around the area. Don't force your gaze at all, just softly focus on an area where you feel intuitively that nature spirits may be.

Now all you are going to do is expand your field of vision to include the astral light, after all, it's everywhere around us. The trick is to keep your eyes focussed in the one direction whilst taking in as much of the area with your peripheral vision as you can.

An added bonus of searching for faeries is that when you begin to see astrally; you will also start to perceive auras. First, you will begin to perceive a gentle haze outlining the trees and plants around you; it's almost as if you are in a daydream.

Once you have this, shift your focus to include as wide a landscape as possible. To begin with, you may only be aware of a sense of movement; almost like a soft flutter in the wind.

As you wait, breathing gently and deeply, you will become aware of small forms surrounded by a soft hazy outline. Don't watch for too long at first; it's necessary for you to build up and strengthen your eyes slowly. If you can practice this exercise during different times of the day and evening, then you will slowly strengthen and expand your astral vision to the point where you should be able to see astrally whenever you wish.

A great exercise that you can do anytime, even in the comfort of your own living room, is to try to see the electromagnetic field, or aura, around your own hand. The more exercise you do, the greater your expanded field of light vision will become.

Just hold your hand, fingers pointed upward, about arms length in front of you. Keep your eyes focussed near the knuckle of your central finger then slowly let your gaze take in the outline of your hand.

After a minute or so you should begin to perceive a soft outline; remember not to stare and to blink naturally. This should be a gradual process and not a trick of the light, or squinting with your eyes to achieve the desired result.

Once you can view the astral light with ease, the realm of the faeries and nature spirits awaits you!

A faery passed me by last night
its wings were luminescent
a tiny light that lit the night
and left me with a question

If life holds more than we can know
and more than we can see
then why is it we cannot hope
that faeries hold the key

Ilana

*T*he Aura

The aura, or electromagnetic field is the colourful glow that surrounds all living things. In a human, the aura pulsates with life force; changing shape and colour with the mood and health of the person being viewed whereas the aura of a tree or plant has more of a constant, regular emanation.

For those who have practised Astral Vision (see "How to Bring Nature Spirits to Your Garden"), you may have noticed different colours around people you meet. Although reading the body's etheric field is certainly not new, with many people perceiving auras naturally, it's only in the last century that we have been able to capture this field on film. Starting with Nikola Tesla's electrophotography, to Semyon and Valentina Kirlian who struggled to research this new field in Russia around 1939, to the more sophisticated methods of capturing the aura that are now available to us.

Many children up until the age of about five or six also perceive auras naturally and often draw pictures of people with a 'fuzzy' outline. Unfortunately, in most cases this ability disappears as friends and school take over. For the few who retain the ability to see astrally and perceive the aura, it is a complex and fascinating subject.

There are many who believe that illness begins in a person's etheric field and therefore if we can view the aura on a regular basis, we can catch many illnesses before they manifest in the physical.

Colours in the Aura

Red   Strong willed, affectionate,
             vital and giving
             If you see too much red
             there is an imbalance
             The person may be prone
             to nervousness
             Watch the circulatory system

Orange   Wisdom, balance and self control

Yellow   Optimistic, good concentration
             A healthy mind and body

Green   Inner strength – Possibly a teacher
             Peaceful and helpful

Blue   Spiritual, honest, loyal, unselfish
             Can be forgetful

Indigo   Practical, capable
             A person who seeks their own path

Violet   A rarity – Highly evolved
             Spiritual and selfless

Amethyst   A quiet and thoughtful person

Scarlet   Quick tempered, egotistical, proud
               May be too passionate

White   All the colours of the spectrum
               Indicates a creative person
               who values truth

Brown   Illness is attempting
               to pervade the system
               Check the area where the
               brown is situated and cleanse
               the aura immediately

Black   Found in three separate
               and diverse situations

               1:   a person near death

               2:   a person devoid of any
                        redeeming features

               3:   as a darkened area
                        between other colours
                        Disease can enter
                        through these areas
                        Take action immediately
                        and cleanse the aura

*T*ake a Journey to the Astral Realm

Come with me on a fabulous journey to this mystic realm that lies very close to our own. The great astral plane, being the closest in density to our own plane of existence, is used by clairvoyants and psychics and can also be accessed by the occult student by means of astral vision or astral projection.

For those not naturally gifted in the means of sending the astral body out at will, this art can be practiced and attained by most who are willing to put in the effort.

Astral Projection

Begin by making yourself comfortable and relaxed. This can be done either by sitting or lying down in a quiet spot. You might like to try setting the scene first with some candles, incense and some astral travel oil (see Magick and Ritual Supplies for the recipe).

The first step is to close your eyes and imagine that you are flying. Imagine yourself gliding above the trees and across a great expanse of land beneath you. As you become more proficient, try picking up speed. Let your imagination take you across deserts and mountains, along sea shores and across oceans. When you are quite comfortable soaring across the sky, it's time to take the next step.

This 'Astral Doorway' method is probably one of the easiest ways to attain astral projection consciously.

I want you to imagine a tunnel just ahead of you. As you enter the tunnel, you will see that your mind is helping you by illuminating the tunnel walls as you fly past, to let you see the speed at which you are travelling. As you look towards the end of the tunnel, you will notice a doorway. When I first began attempting astral travel, I found that no matter what I did, I couldn't reach the doorway. Every time I would get close, I would suddenly find myself back where I started with the doorway in the distance. Most students of the occult will tell you similar stories. As in my case, it can take some time before the desired result is obtained, but with perseverance this method will become easier the more you practice it.

The Journey

Once out, you will find yourself floating just above your physical body. Take a look at your astral body; it will appear to you to be an exact duplicate of your physical body right down to the 'clothing' you happen to be wearing.

The astral body is attached to the physical by means of a 'silver cord' that can stretch any distance you care to travel. Many people believe that upon the death of the physical body, this cord detaches, permitting the soul to continue its journey without having to return.

Let yourself float gently. Remember, in your astral form movement is attained not by effort, but simply by thought. There is no need to open the door, you will find that it is easy to float right through it (although this can be a little unnerving at first).

Now concentrate on raising your vibrations a little, this can be done simply and easily by clearing your everyday thoughts about work, bills etc and then focussing on lifting yourself up to a place free from worry and strife. When you are in your astral form your thoughts become reality. See it – think it – and you will soon find yourself floating in a world not unlike our own, although colour, sight and sound all appear to be somewhat sharper and brighter than normal.

As you look around you will notice structures, houses, buildings; some in various states of creation. One of the biggest flaws of the souls who pass through this realm on their outward journey is in trying to create a world that is familiar to them.

Look closer and you will notice that some of the structures have 'holes' in them, or are only partially completed. This is because the souls who created them have since moved on and so these 'astral shells' have nothing to hold them together and will eventually disintegrate completely.

Here in the astral plane you will find many wonderful sights; beautiful gardens that would take your breath away with some colours that you have never seen before. Flowers and water that both make a tinkling noise, like music playing when you touch them. Cathedrals painstakingly and loving created by religious souls trying to make the astral realm into their idea of heaven, and of course – The Great Hall of Records, or Akashic Records, which contain the imprint of all deeds, words and actions that have ever taken place. Officially this hall resides on the higher planes but the records can still be accessed here on the astral plane.

Gifted students of the occult, psychics and clairvoyants have been known to access these records to gain an insight into various events that have taken place here on the earth plane.

In this hall of records you will see some 'Higher' beings going about their business. If you stand still and observe for a minute you can actually sense the peaceful emanations that come from these highly evolved souls. It's rare for any of them to bother with an astral traveller, but just to be in their presence for a short time is a boost to your spirit.

Leaving the hall of records you can continue your exploration. Apart from 'astral shells' you will also see creatures that are native to the astral plane. Small winged creatures that resemble faeries and some unusual looking creatures that you might find written of in mythology and sometimes even in fantasy books! It's surprising how many writers get their inspiration from things they have seen on the astral plane (Sometimes even accessed during their dream state).

Raising your vibrations again, by concentrating on the peace and love that emanate from this area, you will find yourself outside a very beautiful and peaceful hall, at the doorway stands an angelic being, glowing brightly. You will not be able to enter this hall, but if you look inside you will find souls at slumber, being guarded by angelic and higher beings. These souls have earned their rest and will slumber here, some for a very short while and some for a long while depending on each persons need.

Obviously if your physical demise was a long and painful one or your life was particularly difficult, you may need more time to rest and become refreshed. Since linear time has no sway on the Astral Plane, all things are measured by requirement rather than time frame.

The Astral Plane has many wonders to explore and it will take you many journeys just to make a small dent in the sub-planes and subdivisions, each one has a unique perspective to offer, but for now, see yourself back in your own room and in a split second, you are there.

You will see your body lying peacefully before you. All you have to do to return to your physical body is to reach out and touch it. A person cannot touch their own body without having the two join together.

That is an occult law.

Remember that astral travel is a privilege, take care to respect this ability at all times.

Happy Travels!

The Ancient Art of Cord Magick

(Knot Magick)

A centuries old practice that has definitely gone out of style, those who have gone through traditional initiation will know the cingulum, the nine foot cord that is knotted and worn with the robe.

With a recurring theme through almost every culture, cord magick or knot magick as it is also known, is a simple and enjoyable excrcise in hand crafting, visualisation and positive thinking.
It's easy to braid a little magick into your day.
You've probably tied a knot to remind yourself of something.

Materials needed can be almost anything, but natural materials are best – ribbons of cotton or silk, cord, rope or embroidery threads work well, use your imagination, the choices are endless.

Braid together three to seven (or more if you are feeling adventurous) of either the same colour or different colours if you prefer. When your cord is complete – hold it in both hands and visualise what you require or what you desire. Then tie the first of three knots.

As you tie the second knot – see what you need in detail, go over it in your mind's eye until it becomes perfectly clear.

As you tie the third knot, the deed is done and whatever you required will now manifest in your life. You can use the cord for decoration in your home, or if you prefer, wait until you have what you require and then dispose of the cord by burying it in the garden.

A Witch's Ladder

A cord with 13 knots, can be used for chanting and/or meditation, to keep track of the number of chants, just move the fingers along to the next knot as you go.

Personalising and Empowering Your Athame

The Athame, is every witch's essential tool. This double edged witch's dagger is traditionally black handled and measures around 32cms or 9 inches in length. It is used to raise and direct energy, to cast circle, cut a spiritual gateway in a circle or to bless an object. If you hang a pendulum from the blade, it will give you extra power when scrying.

Television shows and movies are notorious for portraying the witch with his or her knife drawing blood for all manner of rituals, but in reality, the athame should never cut anything but the air.

If you need to cut herbs use your bolline, the white handled working knife that can also be used to inscribe candles and such.

These days with the modern craft becoming more and more eclectic a variety of colours are beginning to find their way in, as well as different shapes and sizes of athames; from the ornate to the simple, the bejewelled to the plain and stark.

Some witches prefer to use an athame with blunt or rounded edges on the blade so that they never inadvertently do any harm to themselves or anyone else. My own athame has sharp edges. It is a constant reminder to me of the power we possess as witches.

If you have not yet purchased your athame, the best way to go about it is to state your intention to the universe and see where it leads you. You might find one in an occult or antique shop or even at a flea market. It doesn't have to be new, but no matter where it comes from you will need to cleanse it of prior energies by sprinkling it with spring water and then passing it through the four elements – earth, air, fire, water.

If you don't find your athame straight away, don't be in a hurry; sometimes it has to find you and may even come to you from a source you hadn't considered. We are all unique and your athame should become like an extension of yourself, reflecting something of your own personality.

Every Witch should have a working athame, as a right of passage for when you come to be initiated; be that through a coven or through self initiation if you are a solitary.

Make it Your Own

Once cleansed, give your athame its own magickal name, one that inspires you and if there is something that does not appeal to you, then change it. Handles are easily altered by wrapping them in black fabric tape. Beads and semi precious stones can be used to decorate the scabbard (the sheath or cover that protects the blade).

One special stone can be used to great effect on the centre of the hilt, but the best means of empowering your athame is to have it engraved. The most effective form of engraving is to use one of the magickal alphabets such as runes, ogham (the tree alphabet), Hebrew, Sanskrit, hieroglyphs or Theban (The witch's alphabet).

These alphabets, along with special wording can be found in many occult books. What you engrave will depend on your particular tradition, however most have a pentacle and their witch name inscribed into the handle.

Another school of thought is that the actual blade should be inscribed with magickal inscriptions down the left and right sides. You might like to inscribe the name of the archangel Raphael, angel of the east wind that governs the element of air which is represented by the athame. If your tradition has the athame as representing the south and the element of fire, as some do, then inscribe the name of the archangel Michael instead. Sigils of the planets or the elements, triquetras, crescent moons or star signs all look good and will add extra power.

Now it's not likely that your local engraver will have a working knowledge of magickal alphabets, so it's best to take a book along with the wording you want. Carefully draw the lettering or sigils on a piece of paper and then show the engraver where you would like it put or if you have a steady hand, you can do what I did and carefully draw or paint directly onto your athame and ask the engraver to engrave over the top. Then just clean away any excess paint when it has been completed. Of course, it would be a good idea to re-cleanse your athame after it has been engraved to remove the engraver's personal energy.

When not in use, find a suitable spot for your athame, possibly on your altar as a representation of the element of air or on your workspace if you practice your craft without religious overtones. I keep mine sheathed and in my bookcase, amongst my magickal reference books on display behind a glass door which not only looks great and inspires me but it also keeps unwanted hands from inadvertently picking it up. No one else should touch your athame but you, unless of course, they have your permission.

Try to make use of it as much as possible so that it feels natural and comfortable in your hands and to help build up as much power as you can.

Magickal and Ritual Supplies

The best thing you can do for yourself is to create a special place for your magickal and ritual supplies. A cupboard is good, however, if you don't have one you can make use of, then use a suitcase or even a large box. There is nothing worse than searching around for candles, herbs, mojo bags, etc. when you are ready to create some magick.

A well stocked Witch's pantry should have the following items:

- Candles: Various colours
- Incense: One to cleanse, one to protect, one to bless - check the Materia Magicka
- Mojo bags and pouches: Sew them yourself for added power; velvet, satin, or cotton, with a black drawstring
- Parchment and papers
- Pen and ink, envelopes
- Small potion bottles and jars: Glass is best, with lids or corks
- An assortment of ribbons, cords and feathers

- Dried Herbs: Although there are literally hundreds to choose from you don't have to go wild. I would start with a few magickal staples like:
  Rose Petals, Lavender, Yarrow, Mugwort and Tonka Beans and perhaps add a couple of the more exotic and rare herbs later. Personally I gather fresh herbs from my garden or from the local herb shop which I get in on the day I intend to use them, however there is nothing wrong with dried herbs, in fact they are definitely better for mojo bags.
- Carrier Oil: Like Sweet Almond or Apricot Kernel oil, some form of vegetable based oil
- Pure Water: Best taken from a natural source, like spring water or water that you have gathered after a thunderstorm (very powerful).
- Salt: Celtic sea salt, or rock crystals
- Crystals: Start with Clear Quartz (healing) Amethyst (spiritual) Rose Quartz (love, calm), Tiger's Eye (focus). You can add more in time.
- Four Magickal Must Have's: No Witch's Pantry would be complete without these four magickal staples that you should make up yourself:
  Anointing Oil, Astral Travel Oil, Magickal Potpourri and Magickal Smelling Salts.

Anointing Oil

On the Full Moon:

Half fill a small potion bottle with a carrier oil

Like Sweet Almond or Apricot Kernel

(any vegetable based oil will do)

Add to this 6 drops of Jasmine oil

for spirituality and balance

3 drops of Myrrh for magick

blessings and consecration

For candles, start in the middle

and work your way out towards the ends

leave the wick

Astral Travel Oil

ENOUGH FOR 7 JOURNEYS
TO THE ASTRAL LIGHT

This oil can be made anytime,

but the waxing moon is best

You will need seven drops of each oil

Jasmine for Projection

Sage for wisdom on the journey

Sandalwood to achieve your goal

Frankincense for protection

An oil burner

Add spring water to the well of your oil burner

To this add 4 drops of your blended astral travel oil

then sit back, close your eyes and fly

Magickal Potpourri

Place in a room when you want to exude magick
This mix is all you will need

In a silken bag or a potpourri dish
place equal parts of the following:

Lavender – For Luck

Rose Petals – For love

Sage – For Wisdom

Willow – For Insight

Cinnamon sticks – To welcome

Thyme – To invite the sidhe

Rosemary – To Remember

Make a small tag with the ingredients listed
and tie the tag to the bag with a gold ribbon
Makes a wonderful gift
for another person of magick
Perhaps for a new Priestess
or for a Handfasting
as they will truly appreciate the effort

Magickal Smelling Salts

Take 3 small jars with lids
Fill them with rock salt
(this salt will hold its shape
even when covered in liquid)

To the first jar, add 5 drops of Lavender oil
Inhale when you need to calm the mind
To aid sleep or clear a headache

To the second jar, add 5 drops of Orange oil
Will energize and clear the mind
Take to work with you and leave on your desk
To give you a boost during the day

To the third jar, add 5 drops of Myrrh oil for magick
Use before any magickal undertakings
To unlock the third eye and open the door
to the magickal world

To Kindle the Magickal Flame

I can remember clearly the moment that would set me on a path apart from the everyday world; The Crooked Path! It was a Tuesday in September, around midday and I had accompanied my mother on an errand to pick up some special herbs from the three old ladies that lived on the corner block in an old ramshackle house with an overgrown garden.

I was about 8 years old. It was 1969 and man had just walked on the moon. People were striving to find themselves and for the first time ever, different paths and different ideas were coming to the fore. Remember this was Australia, we experienced the 60's about ten years after everyone else in the world.

Now my family could never be considered your 'average' family unit. We weren't Gypsies, but we lived like them, constantly on the move, living off our wits. My mother would rather have died a hundred deaths than visit a doctor for anything and made sure she always had a well stocked herb pantry for the small ailments that came our way. As a child growing up in a transient existence, no steady income, no home and very few possessions should have been something of a harrowing experience, but I can honestly say, although we had no worldly goods, we were loved and cared for. In our house we practiced herbal healing, astral travel and psycho kinetic ability.

One of my favourite games was trying to place a thought in another family members mind to have them say or do a certain thing and my father and I would sit for ages concentrating our thoughts on the task at hand. My mother read palms; she had a real knack for it and I can remember the people coming to whatever house we were renting with looks like startled rabbits; half excited and half scared of what they might be told.

My mother was a kind and positive person; I think she helped a lot of souls, most of whom were scared of their own shadows and who probably thought we were – well, I'm not sure what they thought we were. Certainly we never used the word witch or magic but I guess it was always there; hanging in the air. My grandmother who died when I was only 12 years old, was to me a bit of a mean old woman. Although she'd had seven children of her own, I don't think she liked children at all. She certainly had no time for them, or me.

The only good memories I have of her were seeing her in the garden growing her beloved herbs, or in the kitchen. Oh my, that woman could cook! Then, of course, there was her fabulous Book of Secrets. I got to look in it (look, but never touch) whenever she took it out to make up any kind of formula or potion for whatever ailed us.

We were of a Jewish heritage, but my grandmother was pure Celt. She had a broad Scottish accent, although her people were originally from Ireland. Born on the ship taking her mother and father from Ireland to Scotland, she had all of the Celtic fire within her and luckily for us, all of the old folk remedies as well, learned from her own mother. With these proud bloodlines running through our veins, it's no wonder we were wanderers, healers and seekers of truth and light. "It's in the blood" she used to say.

By the time I was 8 years old, I had come to understand that other children didn't play the same games that I did. Mostly, they didn't know what I was talking about and just looked at me blankly. Their mother's never taught them about seeing a person's aura or calling the faery folk to the garden.

On very rare occasions I would wish to be like everyone else, but deep down inside I knew that a life without faeries and astral travel and all the other wonderful things that we knew about, wouldn't be worth living. So I held my tongue and learned to "be silent".

On this particular day, I can remember being somewhat petulant. I was bored and I couldn't think of anything to do. I was being a brat; whining as we went along. As we approached the door of the old house it was opened by an old lady with bright pink cheeks and a sweet smile on her face.

Looking back, she was probably only fifty or so, but to an eight year old that's practically dead! And of course, everyone looked older in the sixties.

In Australia, ladies still wore white gloves and prim suits when they went to town, along with hats or their hair in buns. There was no individuality or colour to the world. You complied or you ostracised.

The lady greeted my mother warmly and ushered her inside and down the hallway with its imposing photographs in heavy frames and into the sitting room. It was a friendly room; big soft seats with embroidered cushions and I can remember lots of candles, candles everywhere; some of them in big, impressive holders. I was told to sit in here whilst my mother conducted her business.

I sat on the lounge with my feet dangling and watched as my mother was taken through to the sunroom with the large wooden table. I can remember there were flowers everywhere and all sorts of herbs and plants sitting on the shelves and hanging from the wooden rafters. Due to the open plan of the rooms I could see her clearly from my vantage point on the lounge. I liked this place, it had a good 'feel' to it. So I sat quietly and watched as my mother handed over her list of requirements.

As the nice woman left to gather the herbs on the list, two others entered the room and after greeting my mother warmly they sat down with her at the table and all three started talking intently. I wasn't really listening, being engrossed by the beautiful plants and flowers that seemed to fill every space within the sunroom. "How wonderful to live here", I thought to myself.

When the older woman returned she was carrying a brown paper bag and handed it over to my mother who thanked her and paid the money; then to my surprise I was ushered into the room and told to sit at the table next to my mother.

Mum squeezed my hand and told me I was in for a treat. I hoped it was fairy cakes and lemonade, but it would turn out to be something far more earth shattering and life altering. This was the moment that I was to see magick, real magick, come to life. Certainly I was no stranger to the magickal world. Even at age 8, I knew how to cast a circle of protection. I understood that life had so much more to offer than we could see, touch or feel. My entire family had some psychic ability and I myself possessed a kinetic ability that came and went at the oddest times and would be something that even to this day, I would have no control over; but this was different. This was real, purposeful, intentional magick, powerful and under control. You could positively feel it in the air!

On the table stood a large wrought iron candlestick holder with one tall candle standing proudly in the centre. Candle wax in diverse colours dripped around the holder, cascading like a wax fountain down to its base. As I looked around the table I could see that each of the women, including my mother, were staring intently at the candle, slowly an almost inaudible chant began; rhythmic and somehow soothing to the ears. As the chant grew louder, I saw two of the women rocking back and forth whilst the third began making strange movements with her hands. Suddenly, the candle in the middle of the table came to life, bursting into flame as if on queue.

I know my mouth fell open, I could feel my mother glance down at me, but I was far too interested in what was happening to take any notice. The women smiled and looked at me; the oldest giving me a knowing wink and then they proceeded with the meeting as if nothing momentous had just happened!

My mother and I stayed for another half hour or so before we left to Continue our day. I can remember pestering her to tell me what had just happened, but all she would say was that life held more questions than it did answers and I should never be surprised by what might be possible.

From that moment onwards I was hooked. I would spend the next 40 odd years seeking, learning and finding my own way through a veritable sea of differing paths. Some were brilliant and enlightening, others were pure wind and bluster, but from each I would glean whatever I could before moving on.

I have attained third degree (twice), become a student of the Kabbalah and of high magick and finally, now, at age 53, I have come to understand something of the crooked path. You really DO have to do it your way. It is a path that can be shown, but not lived by anyone but you. So many people will try to tell you that their way is the only way to do a certain thing, but the truth is, there is always another way. Take the parts that feel right to you and make them your own and most important of all -Make sure you find the joy and the wonder in whatever you do because this is what causes the magick to occur.

Don't let anyone or any group suck the joy out of learning the Craft, for joyous it truly is. I found my joy in learning the magickal arts and occult laws, in becoming an artist, a scribe and an herbalist. These things please me, like my love of the ocean, trees and animals, but most of all I love the mysteries and wonders that life holds and because of that I will always be a seeker of truth and light.

The learning never ends.

As for the candle lighting – I found out for myself many years later several ways to "Light the Magickal Flame". I now know that the women conjured the element of fire and the high priestess took that energy and threw it at the candle wick to make it ignite.

My personal favourite is learning how to "breathe" the elements so that when you blow on the candle wick, it comes into flame. It always looks so impressive, but here is the one I want to share with you now.

First, try this simple experiment.

Light a candle and then blow out the flame. Whilst the smoke is drifting upwards take a match and strike it, then hold the flame 2 or 3 inches above the unlit wick. The smoke will carry the flame to the wick and then ignite it without you touching it, just like magick!

You will be using this same method, but without the smoke. Instead the flame will travel along the line that you build with your mind.

Give it a try, you might surprise yourself; the method is easy.

Stand two candles in their holders about 4 inches apart. Light one of the candles and then sit yourself in a chair back about 9 feet from them. Now see the flame from the lit candle running across to the unlit wick. See it in your mind's eye. Squint your eyes if it helps. Build a bridge, a line of flame.

You can use the first candle to light the second.

A FINAL WORD
To Dare, To Will, To Keep Silent

These were the words I learned whilst growing up. These days young witches don't have to keep as silent as we did. The wheel has indeed turned, which is a good thing, but remember that magick –real magick will always be for the few and not the many. If you are one of the lucky ones who has chosen the crooked path, or had it choose you, then know that your path will change and alter and grow year after year, as it should.

Learn all that you can, by book or by teacher and remember to honour where you came from. I know many witches who practise their craft within the confines of their family's respective religions or belief systems. If this works for you and keeps the peace, then fine.

Some witches prefer to practise their craft without religious overtones and use a workspace instead of an altar. The craft itself has expanded and diversified to the point where there are so many different paths to choose from, you will no doubt find one that suits your needs.

I currently work as a scribe for a magickal coven, but spend the majority of my time as a solitary. I class myself as a green witch, using the term green in the old Celtic manner (as in green man, green wood etc.) In other words, I honour the earth and the animals, all of nature, the elementals and the Source of all that is – Goddess/God, whatever that means to you – and I use the herbs, trees and flowers, all the bounty of the earth in my crafting.

I choose not to use the pantheon of Gods and Goddesses in my craft, both in deference to my heritage and simply because I have never felt the need. I would class myself as a very spiritual person with a great love of nature and an all consuming thirst for esoteric knowledge.

More than anything the Craft has taught me that NOTHING is impossible. Seek the light and the truth and find the beauty wherever you can.

I know a lot of modern witches don't use the term Blessed Be anymore, but I must admit I have always had a fondness for it.

So since I am now a crone, with many years of experience and hopefully some wisdom behind me, I will end my book with the age old blessing; who knows, maybe it will come full circle and become fashionable again.

May the faeries dance around you
And magick light your path -
Blessed Be!

*I*ndex

About the Author

Ilana Sturm is an artist, author and witch born in Australia to a family filled with magick, lore and tradition. Over the last 30 plus years she has studied and practiced many different magickal disciplines and traditions that have all contributed to her own personal crooked path.

Her journey has led her from the pyramids of Egypt to Stonehenge, from Glastonbury Tor to Uluru and beyond. She now spends her time at her home by the sea where she paints, grows herbs and continues her writing, hoping to pass on to the next generation some of the wisdoms she learned on the way.

Also by Ilana Sturm

The 13th Moon . . . . Pendraig Publishing
Idris and the Scroll of Destiny . . Pendraig Publishing
Contributor: Call of the God . . . . . . TDM Publishing
The Witch in the Mirror . . . . Coming soon

www.ingramcontent.com/pod-product-compliance
Lightning Source LLC
Chambersburg PA
CBHW051950090426
42741CB00008B/1329